LEAVE
THE GUN,
TAKE THE
CANNOLI

LEAVE THE GUN, TAKE THE CANNOLI

A Wiseguy's Guide to the Workplace

Kurt Luchs

BARNES
&NOBLE
BOOKS
NEW YORK

This edition published by Barnes & Noble, Inc., by arrangement
with becker&mayer!

Copyright © 2003 by Kurt Luchs.

Leave the Gun, Take the Cannoli is produced by
becker&mayer!, Ltd., Bellevue, Washington
www.beckermayer.com

Editorial: Kate Hall
Design: Joanna Price
Production coordination: Cindy Lashley
Project management: Sheila Kamuda

Printed in China.

ISBN 0-7607-4575-7

Library of Congress Cataloging-in-Publication data is available.

M 10 9 8 7 6 5 4 3 2 1

CONTENTS

INTRODUCTION

You probably know me as America's foremost business guru, the author of motivational bestsellers like *Who Moved My "Who Moved My Cheese" Book?*, *Swimming with Inflatable Sharks*, and *Good to Great Depression: Seven Ways to Make the Collapse of the World Economy Work for You*. If you bought any of my earlier books, I thank you—and I also pity you, because they have all been rendered useless by this one, my magnum opus.

You see, in scouring the globe for the most valuable business strategies, I was looking for the love of money in all the wrong places. Sure, the owners and managers of the great multinational corporations love money. They love it enough to steal, lie, and cheat for it . . . but so few of them love it enough to kill for it.

That's what separates them from the real business geniuses—the men who run the Mafia. These guys will kill for money. They know how to make it—and how to keep it. Not one of them has ever filed a corporate tax return or issued a shareholder's report, and yet profits roll in year after year. You want to see how a real business organization runs? Look at organized crime. You want real business wisdom? Ask a wiseguy. Problem is, he won't tell you, and if he did, he'd have to kill you.

Fortunately, I am under no such constraint. I spent the last few years studying the ways of the Mafia, the mob, the Cosa Nostra, or whatever you want to call it. I read police reports, court transcripts, the screenplays for all three *Godfather* movies, and other vital wiseguy documents. I even talked to Vinny down at the cigar store (whenever he wasn't on the phone to his bookie). Then I entered the Witness Protection Program to write this book, which brings you all of the greatest gems of wiseguy strategy in one convenient volume.

Unfortunately, many wiseguy sayings and ideas are convoluted—some would say "twisted"—and hard to understand. That's why I've thoughtfully provided explanations after each bit of advice. Let's face it: If you were already wise, you wouldn't need to listen to real wiseguys like these. But it's never too late to wise up and start moving up your own corporate ladder! Let the lessons begin.

—Kurt Luchs

Chapter 1
CHOOSING A CAREER

As far back as I can remember, I always wanted to
be a gangster.

—HENRY HILL, *Goodfellas* (1990)

☞ **Your deepest and oldest dreams are
your best motivators.**

What do you mean "gangsters?" It's *business*.

—WALLY, *Force of Evil* (1948)

☞ **True then, true today.**

MICHAEL SULLIVAN: He murdered Annie and Peter.

JOHN ROONEY: There are only murderers in this room.

Michael, open your eyes! This is the life we chose, the life we lead.

And there is only one guarantee: None of us will see heaven.

—*Road to Perdition* (2002)

☞ **Forget heaven. Concentrate on seeing retirement.**

Twenty dwarves took turns doing handstands on the carpet.

—BUGSY SIEGEL, *Bugsy* (1991)

☞ **And if they did it in front of the right manager, rest assured they all got hired.**

No questions. No answers. That's the business we're in.
You accept it and move on.

—VINCENT, *Ronin* (1998)

☞ **If you have time to ask why, they're not keeping you busy enough down at the office.**

MEADOW SOPRANO: Are you in the Mafia?

ANTHONY "TONY" SOPRANO, SR.: Am I in the what?!

MEADOW SOPRANO: Whatever you want to call it.
Organized crime.

—*The Sopranos* ("College," Season 1)

☞ **Or business. Same thing.**

MAX: You'll carry that stink of the streets with you the rest of
your life.
NOODLES: I like the stink of the streets. It makes me feel good.
I like the smell. It opens up my lungs. And, it gives me a hard-on.
—*Once Upon a Time in America* (1984)

☞ **With a work environment this enticing,
your career choice practically makes itself.**

Oh for Pete's sake. Oh for Pete's sake, he's fleeing the interview!
He's fleeing the interview!
—MARGE GUNDERSON, *Fargo* (1996)

☞ **Not all applicants will be equally interested
in the position.**

MAY EMMERICH: Oh Lon, when I think of all those awful people you come in contact with—downright criminals—I get scared.

ALONZO EMMERICH: Oh, there's nothing so different about them. After all, crime is only . . . a left-handed form of human endeavor.

—*The Asphalt Jungle* (1950)

☞ **Whereas business is a left-handed form of human endeavor where everybody has two left hands, and the first left hand doesn't know what the other left hand is doing.**

Chapter 2
GETTING AHEAD: TIPS FOR SUCCESS

I can't face the world in the morning. I must have coffee before
I can speak.

—UNCLE CHARLIE, *Shadow of a Doubt* (1943)

☞ **Breakfast is not the most important meal
of the day—coffee is.**

SAM: Whenever there is any doubt, there is no doubt. That's
the first thing they teach you.

VINCENT: Who taught you?

SAM: I don't remember. That's the second thing they teach you.

—*Ronin* (1998)

☞ **The third thing they teach you is: You
only need to know those first two things
they taught you.**

Oh boy! With me, being smart is a disease!

—WALLY FAY, *Mildred Pierce* (1945)

☞ **You'll wish others shared your disease, but you'll find that in business, intelligence is not very contagious.**

JOE COLLINS: I don't care about everybody else.

GALLAGHER: That's cemetery talk.

JOE COLLINS: Why not, we're buried, ain't we? Only thing is, we ain't dead.

—*Brute Force* (1947)

☞ **Stay in a dead-end job, and you will be . . .**

Made it, Ma! Top of the world!

[Sudden explosion kills Jarrett]

—CODY JARRETT, *White Heat* (1949)

> Watch out—when success does come, it may blow up in your face.

You like money. You got a great big dollar sign there where most women have a heart.

—JOHNNY CLAY, *The Killing* (1956)

> On the other hand, a dollar sign will never require a bypass.

The ones that say they don't want anything always get more in
the end.

—ANN NEWTON, *Shadow of a Doubt* (1943)

☞ **Unfortunately, this is only true of unwanted
additional work, not of raises.**

I can afford a blemish on my character, but not on my clothes.

—SHELBY CARPENTER, *Laura* (1944)

☞ **However, no one has yet found a way to
dry-clean your character.**

I want him dead! I want his family dead! I want his house burnt to the ground! I want to go there in the middle of the night and piss on his ashes!

—AL CAPONE, *The Untouchables* (1987)

☞ **Anything worth doing is worth doing right . . . but you may have to put in a little overtime.**

VIVIAN: Why did you have to go on?

PHILIP MARLOWE: Too many people told me to stop.

—*The Big Sleep* (1946)

☞ **Follow orders and you'll go far. Don't follow them and you'll go a lot farther.**

[Tony disapproves of Meadow's new boyfriend because he is black]

CARMELA SOPRANO: You want her to be with him, just keep it up. Keep playing the race card. You're gonna drive her right into his arms.

ANTHONY "TONY" SOPRANO, SR.: Not if I cut off those fuckin' arms.

—*The Sopranos* ("Proshai, Livushka," Season 3)

☞ **Always have a backup plan.**

My, my, my. Such a lot of guns around town and so few brains!

—PHILIP MARLOWE, *The Big Sleep* (1946)

☞ **Power and intelligence are almost always inversely proportional.**

The main thing is to *have* the money. I've been rich, and I've been poor. Believe me, rich is better.

—DEBBY MARSH, *The Big Heat* (1953)

☞ **Money can't make you happy . . . but it sure makes being unhapppy more pleasant!**

TEITTLEMAN: Do you have a daughter, Mr. Soprano?

ANTHONY "TONY" SOPRANO, SR.: Yes. Call me Tony.

TEITTLEMAN: What would you do if your daughter was abused by her husband?

ANTHONY "TONY" SOPRANO, SR.: Talk to him—

SILVIO DANTE: Yeah, [with] a ball peen hammer.

—*The Sopranos* ("Denial, Anger, Acceptance," Season 1)

☞ **You can't do the job right without the proper tools.**

This country, you gotta make the money first. Then when you get the money, you get the power. Then when you get the power, then you get the woman.

—TONY MONTANA, *Scarface* (1983)

☞ **Go after the woman first and you'll never get the money or the power . . . or the woman.**

In my case, self-absorption is completely justified. I have never discovered any other subject quite so worthy of my attention.

—WALDO LYDECKER, *Laura* (1944)

☞ **Focus on what you love.**

Well then, you just fulfilled the first rule of law enforcement:
Make sure when your shift is over you go home alive. Here endeth
the lesson.

—JIM MALONE, *The Untouchables* (1987)

☛ **Before trying to keep your goals in front of
you, keep your behind safe.**

ORDELL ROBBIE: You know you smoke too much of that shit.
That shit's gonna rob you of your ambition.
MELANIE: Not if your ambition is to get high and watch TV.

—*Jackie Brown* (1997)

☛ **So remember to aim high . . . or to get high
. . . or anyway, to watch lots of TV.**

[Stealing a car]

BONNIE PARKER: Hey, that ain't ours!

CLYDE BARROW: Sure it is.

BONNIE PARKER: But we come in this one.

CLYDE BARROW: That don't mean we have to go home in it!

—*Bonnie and Clyde* (1967)

 **Seize opportunities.**

Your enemies always get strong on what you leave behind.

—MICHAEL CORLEONE, *The Godfather III* (1990)

 **You *can* take your authority and your perks with you—you must, if your career is to grow.**

LEO O'BANNION: So you wanna kill 'im.

EDDIE DANE: For starters.

—*Miller's Crossing* (1990)

☞ **Well begun is half done.**

All you can do is pray for a quick death, which you ain't going to get.

—MR. BLONDE, *Reservoir Dogs* (1992)

☞ **Aim high anyway.**

You should never underestimate the predictability
of stupidity.

—BULLET TOOTH TONY, *Snatch* (2001)

☞ **And it makes planning so much easier.**

[Debby surveys Bannion's undistinguished hotel room]

Say, I like this. Early nothing!

—DEBBY MARSH, *The Big Heat* (1953)

☞ **Your decor should match your ambition.**

TOM REAGAN: All in all not a bad guy—if looks, brains, and personality don't count.

VERNA: You better hope they don't.

—*Miller's Crossing* (1990)

They don't.

DANNY: Thirteen million and you drive this piece of shit cross country to pick me up?

RUSTY: Blew it all on the suit.

—*Ocean's Eleven* (2001)

Dress for success. But if you paid thirteen million for a suit, you need to learn something about buying wholesale.

We can stop, get pancakes, and then we'll get laid.

—CARL SHOWALTER, *Fargo* (1996)

☞ **A good plan is a simple plan.**

You see, the only man that's not afraid to die is the man that's dead already.

—CHARLIE STROM, *The Killers* (1964)

☞ **Or, a guy who calls God "Dad."**

Chapter 3
GETTING ALONG WITH YOUR BOSS

Why are you makin' me do this, you fat, fuckin', miserable piece a' shit?!

—ANTHONY "TONY" SOPRANO, SR.,

The Sopranos ("Funhouse," Season 2)

☞ **Don't be afraid to question your boss.**

Check out the big brain on Brett!

—JULES, *Pulp Fiction* (1994)

☞ **Obviously, Brett is not management material.**

In Vegas, everybody's gotta watch everybody else. Since the players are looking to beat the casino, the dealers are watching the players. The box men are watching the dealers. The floor men are watching the box men. The pit bosses are watching the floor men. The shift bosses are watching the pit bosses. The casino manager is watching the shift bosses. I'm watching the casino manager. And the eye-in-the-sky is watching us all.

—ACE ROTHSTEIN, *Casino* (1995)

☞ **In wiseguy philosophy, God is not the Unseen Mover, He's the Unseen Security Camera.**

Good for you. Don't take no shit off nobody!

—JIMMY CONWAY, *Goodfellas* (1990)

☞ **On the other hand, if that nobody is actually "somebody" . . . maybe you better take it.**

If he were mean or vicious, or if he'd bawl me out or something, I'd like him better.

—KITTY MARCH, *Scarlet Street* (1945)

☞ **A good boss is no good—for a masochist.**

If anything in this life is certain, if history has taught us anything, it's that you can kill anyone.

—MICHAEL CORLEONE, *The Godfather II* (1974)

☞ **Don't despair over bad bosses and worthless (but protected) coworkers or employees. Rome wasn't built in a day . . . and the worst Roman emperors weren't assassinated in a day, either.**

TESS: You know what your problem is?

DANNY: I only have one?

—*Ocean's Eleven* (2001)

☞ **Always view criticism in the most positive light.**

When you kill a king, you don't stab him in the dark.

You kill him where the entire court can watch him die.

—AMSTERDAM VALLON, *Gangs of New York* (2002)

☞ **If your boss is crummy, don't stab him in the back; stab him in the front.**

I'm serious as a heart attack.

—ORDELL ROBBIE, *Jackie Brown* (1997)

☞ **And if he's like most bosses, he's even more likely to take years off your life.**

I don't give a good fuck what you know or don't know, but I'm
going to torture you anyway.

—MR. BLONDE, *Reservoir Dogs* (1992)

☞ **Know your supervisor's ground rules up-front.**

You know what he'll do when he finds out, dontcha? Beat my
teeth out, then kick me in the stomach for mumbling.

—PHILIP MARLOWE, *The Big Sleep* (1946)

☞ **And dock your pay for getting blood on
his shoes.**

Haven't you bothered me enough, you big banana-head?

—ANGELA PHINLAY, *The Asphalt Jungle* (1950)

☞ **That's Mr. Banana-Head to you.**

But, I'm funny how? I mean, funny like I'm a clown? I amuse you? I make you laugh?

—TOMMY DEVITO, *Goodfellas* (1990)

☞ **The difference is, clowns make you laugh
until you die; they don't make you die
for laughing.**

ORDELL ROBBIE: Fuck is wrong with you, knockin' on the door like the goddamn police? You lookin' to get shot?

MAX CHERRY: I thought you might be asleep.

ORDELL ROBBIE: You keep fuckin' with me, you the one gonna be asleep forever.

—*Jackie Brown* (1997)

☞ **Listen to your boss closely to catch those ever-so-subtle warnings.**

He told them to look not at the facts, but at the meaning of the facts. Then he said the facts had no meaning.

—ED CRANE, *The Man Who Wasn't There* (2001)

☞ **If only all managerial directives were so clear.**

Here come the pain!

—CARLITO, *Carlito's Way* (1993)

☞ **Everyone should have a mantra with which to celebrate the beginning of the work day.**

He's rich! Do you understand? He thinks he can get away with anything!

—JAKE GITTES, *Chinatown* (1974)

☞ **Guess what? He's right.**

Chapter 4
GETTING ALONG
WITH YOUR COWORKERS

JOEL CAIRO: You always have a very smooth explanation ready.

SAM SPADE: What do you want me to do, learn to stutter?

—*The Maltese Falcon* (1941)

☞ **Go the extra mile to accommodate your coworkers.**

Well, you can't trust Melanie, but you can always trust Melanie to be Melanie.

—ORDELL ROBBIE, *Jackie Brown* (1997)

☞ **And that's the only kind of trust you need to have with your coworkers.**

If I'd been a ranch, they would have named me the Bar Nothing.

—GILDA, *Gilda* (1946)

There's one in every office. Just make sure you're not the dude who visits her ranch.

Even a broken clock is right twice a day.

—ANTHONY "TONY" SOPRANO, SR.,

  The Sopranos ("Pax Soprana," Season 1)

That means the final score is clock, 2: coworkers, 0.

DIXON STEELE: Go ahead and get some sleep, and we'll have dinner together tonight.

LAUREL GRAY: We'll have dinner tonight. But not together.

—*In a Lonely Place* (1950)

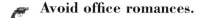 **Avoid office romances.**

Then she tried to sit on my lap while I was standing up.

—PHILIP MARLOWE, *The Big Sleep* (1946)

What *not* to say at the next sexual harassment sensitivity seminar.

DR. JENNIFER MELFI: When's the last time you had a prostate exam?

ANTHONY "TONY" SOPRANO, SR.: Hey, I don't even let anybody wag their finger in my *face.*

—*The Sopranos* ("Pax Soprana," Season 1)

☞ **Respect boundaries.**

EDDIE DANE: How'd you get the fat lip?

TOM REAGAN: Old war welt. Acts up around morons.

—*Miller's Crossing* (1990)

☞ **Don't be afraid to share tidbits from your personal life.**

Why don't you try sticking your head up your ass? See if it fits.

—TONY MONTANA, *Scarface* (1983)

☞ **Your coworkers look to you for creative and helpful suggestions. Don't disappoint them.**

This guy could fuck up a cup of coffee!

—NICKY SANTORO, *Casino* (1995)

☞ **Problem is, he's usually the boss's brother-in-law. What to do? Switch to mineral water.**

VIRGIL MALLOY: Watch it, bud.

TURK MALLOY: Who you calling bud, pal?

VIRGIL MALLOY: Who you calling pal, friend?

TURK MALLOY: Who you calling friend, jackass?!

VIRGIL MALLOY: Don't call me a jackass.

TURK MALLOY: I just did call you a jackass.

—*Ocean's Eleven* (2001)

☞ **The more nicknames, the more affection there is between you and your coworkers.**

JULES: Oh man, I will never forgive yo ass for this shit. This is some fucked-up, repugnant shit!

VINCENT: Jules, did you ever hear the philosophy that once a man admits that he's wrong, then he's immediately forgiven for all wrongdoings? Have you ever heard that?

JULES: Get the fuck out my face with that shit! The mother-fucker said that never had to pick up itty bitty pieces of skull on account of your dumb ass!

—*Pulp Fiction* (1994)

☞ **Sometimes you must confront.**

I'm not sure I agree with you a hundred percent on your police work there, Lou.

—MARGE GUNDERSON, *Fargo* (1996)

👉 Be gentle when correcting others.

Somebody's stickin' a red-hot poker up our ass, and I want to know whose name's on the handle!

—MR. PINK, *Reservoir Dogs* (1992)

👉 Give credit where credit is due.

JOHNNY PRINCE: Lazy Legs *[kisses her]*, I don't know what you told Janeway, but you got him eatin' right out of your hand.

KITTY MARCH: It won't stop with lunch!

—*Scarlet Street* (1945)

☞ **Fraternizing helps build departmental morale.**

VINCE STONE: Hey, that's nice perfume.

DEBBY MARSH: Something new. It attracts mosquitoes and repels men.

—*The Big Heat* (1953)

☞ **Take time to notice the little things about your coworkers.**

It ain't the way I wanted it! I can handle things! I'm smart! Not like everybody says . . . like dumb . . . I'm smart and I want respect!

—FREDO CORLEONE, *The Godfather II* (1974)

☞ **If you're going to model yourself on a Corleone, make sure it's Vito or Michael— not Fredo.**

LEFTY: He's a stand-up guy?

JIMMY: I said I knew him, Left, I didn't say I fucked him.

—*Donnie Brasco* (1997)

☞ **Get to know your coworkers, so long as it isn't in the biblical sense.**

You're dumber than you think I think you are.

—JAKE GITTES, *Chinatown* (1974)

If only smart mattered!

I'm tellin' you, this guy is protected from up on high by the Prince of Darkness.

—JEFF RABIN, *The Usual Suspects* (1995)

The boss always has favorites; make sure they're your favorites, too.

Chapter 5
EFFECTIVE
COMMUNICATION

ORDELL ROBBIE: Is she dead?

LOUIS: I . . . I . . . pretty much.

ORDELL ROBBIE: What do you mean, "pretty much," Louis?
That ain't no fuckin' answer! Yes or no. Is she dead?

LOUIS: I . . . I . . . think so.

—*Jackie Brown* (1997)

☞ **If politicians have taught us anything, it's that
a yes-or-no question is the one kind that
should never be answered yes or no.**

ESMARELDA: And what is your name?

BUTCH: Butch.

ESMARELDA: Butch . . . what does it mean?

BUTCH: I'm American, honey. Our names don't mean shit.

—*Pulp Fiction* (1994)

☛ **Respect cultural differences.**

I'm gonna say a few things, I'm gonna say some bad words, and you're just gonna have to deal with it.

—ANTHONY "TONY" SOPRANO, SR.,

　The Sopranos ("Fortunate Son," Season 3)

☛ **Effective meetings should begin with a summary of the agenda.**

I distrust a close-mouthed man. He generally picks the wrong time to talk and says the wrong things. Talking's something you can't do judiciously, unless you keep in practice. Now, sir, we'll talk if you like. I'll tell you right out, I'm a man who likes talking to a man who likes to talk.

—KASPER GUTMAN, *The Maltese Falcon* (1941)

☞ **Talk is cheap. Don't be afraid of giving it away.**

Me, I always tell the truth. Even when I lie.

—TONY MONTANA, *Scarface* (1983)

☞ **The best way not to be caught in a lie is never to tell one. If you need to deceive, always do it with the truth.**

[Chris and Paulie just botched a hit on a Russian gangster and are lost in the woods. Tony calls and gets bad reception]

ANTHONY "TONY" SOPRANO, SR.: The guy you're looking for is an ex-commando. He killed sixteen Chechen rebels single-handed.

PAULIE "WALNUTS" GUALTIER: Get the fuck outta here.

ANTHONY "TONY" SOPRANO, SR.: Yeah, nice, huh? He was with the interior ministry. Guy's some kind of Russian green beret. This guy cannot come back to tell this story. You understand?

PAULIE "WALNUTS" GUALTIER: I hear you.

ANTHONY "TONY" SOPRANO, SR.: *[breaking up]* I'm serious, Paulie.

PAULIE "WALNUTS" GUALTIER: Ton? Ton, you there? *[hangs up]* You're not going to believe this. He killed sixteen Czechoslovakians. Guy was an interior decorator.

CHRISTOPHER MOLTISANTI: His house looked like shit.

—*The Sopranos* ("Pine Barrens," Season 3)

☞ **A good communicator is a good listener.**

JULES: Hey, sewer rat may taste like pumpkin pie but I'd never know 'cause I wouldn't eat the filthy motherfuckers. Pigs sleep and root in shit. That's a filthy animal. I ain't eat nothin' that ain't got enough sense to disregard its own feces.

VINCENT: How about a dog? Dog eats his own feces.

JULES: I don't eat dog either.

VINCENT: Yeah, but do you consider a dog to be a filthy animal?

JULES: I wouldn't go so far as to call a dog filthy but they're definitely dirty. But, dog's got personality. Personality goes a long way.

VINCENT: Ah, so by that rationale, if a pig had a better personality, he'd cease to be a filthy animal. Is that true?

JULES: Well we'd have to be talkin' about one charmin' mother-fuckin' pig. I mean he'd have to be ten times more charmin' than that Arnold on *Green Acres*, you know what I'm sayin'?

—*Pulp Fiction* (1994)

☛ **Some brainstorming sessions are more productive than others.**

[Into a mirror]

You talkin' to me? You talking to me? You talkin' to me? Then who the hell else are you talkin'—you talkin' to me? Well I'm the only one here. Who the fuck do you think you're talking to? Oh, yeah? Huh? 'Kay.

—TRAVIS BICKLE, *Taxi Driver* (1976)

Practice your presentations in front of a mirror. You'll find you're a very tough audience.

You learned the two greatest things in life: Never rat on your friends and *always* keep your mouth shut.

—JIMMY CONWAY, *Goodfellas* (1990)

Interesting corollary: If you observe the second rule, you never have to worry about the first.

PAULIE "WALNUTS" GUALTIER: How 'bout you? You remember your first blowjob?

SILVIO DANTE: Yeah, of course.

PAULIE "WALNUTS" GUALTIER: How long did it take for the guy to come?

—*The Sopranos* ("Toodle-Fucking-Oo," Season 2)

☞ **Don't be too quick to agree until you know what the other guy's actually saying.**

[Mr. Blonde has cut off Marvin's ear and begins talking into it]

Hey, what's goin' on? You hear that?

—MR. BLONDE, *Reservoir Dogs* (1992)

☞ **Take care to speak clearly and audibly.**

[Jules shoots the guy on the couch during Brett's interrogation]

Oh, I'm sorry. Did I break your concentration? I didn't mean to do that. Please, continue.

—JULES, *Pulp Fiction* (1994)

☞ **When their attention wanders, gently but firmly return them to the topic at hand.**

TESS: You're a thief and a liar.

DANNY: I only lied about being a thief, and I don't do that anymore.

TESS: Steal?

DANNY: Lie.

—*Ocean's Eleven* (2001)

☞ **Always be clear about what exactly you're taking responsibility for.**

All I have in this world is my balls and my word, and I don't break 'em for no one. You understand?

—TONY MONTANA, *Scarface* (1983)

☞ **Don't worry—in the workplace there's always someone else ready and willing to break your balls for you.**

Never let anyone know what you're thinking.

—MICHAEL CORLEONE, *The Godfather III* (1990)

☞ **Or feeling, for that matter.**

Chapter 6
JOB DESCRIPTIONS

GREGOR: Can't we do something?

SAM: We are doing something, we're sitting here waiting.

—*Ronin* (1998)

> It may not look good on a résumé, but that's your job description ninety percent of the time.

One way or another, we all work for our vice.

—DOC, *The Asphalt Jungle* (1950)

> Or, as the case may be, our corporate vice president.

NORRIS: Are you attempting to tell me my duties, sir?

PHILIP MARLOWE: No, just having fun trying to guess what they are.

—*The Big Sleep* (1946)

☞ **If everyone knows exactly what you're supposed to do, they also know exactly what you're *not* supposed to do, and that can be very limiting.**

We rob banks!

—BONNIE PARKER, *Bonnie and Clyde* (1967)

☞ **Take pride in what you do.**

You a gangster now. You on the other side. Whole new ballgame.
You can't learn about it in school and you can't have a late start.

—CARLITO, *Carlito's Way* (1993)

☛ **However, the hours are good, and look at the benefits!**

KEATON: I'm a businessman.

COP: Yeah? What's that, the restaurant business? No.
From now on you're in the gettin'-fucked-by-us business.

—*The Usual Suspects* (1995)

☛ **Not all changes in your job will be improvements.**

Chapter 7

OFFICE POLITICS, OFFICE ETIQUETTE

CALLOWAY: You don't know what you're mixing in. Get the next plane.

MARTINS: As soon as I get to the bottom of this, I'll get the next plane.

CALLOWAY: Death's at the bottom of everything, Martins. Leave death to the professionals.

—*The Third Man* (1939)

☞ **Incidentally, the professionals are not consultants. Consultants are the people the incompetents hire to kill the professionals.**

I don't like violence, Tom. I'm a businessman. Blood is a big expense.

—SOLOZZO, *The Godfather* (1972)

☞ **It'll also ruin that nice new carpeting in your office.**

GENERAL STERNWOOD: How do you like your brandy, sir?

PHILIP MARLOWE: In a glass.

—*The Big Sleep* (1946)

☞ **Desk drawer flasks are *so* over!**

A wiseguy never pays for his drinks.

—LEFTY, *Donnie Brasco* (1997)

☞ **And an even wiser guy never drinks on the job.**

WALTER BROWN: You make me sick to my stomach.

MRS. NEALL: Well, use your own sink.

—*The Narrow Margin* (1952)

☞ **Interdepartmental cooperation is a joy to behold.**

He never asks a second favor when he's been refused the first. Understood?

—TOM HAGEN, *The Godfather* (1972)

☞ **Determine quickly who your enemies are and who your friends are . . . and waste no time trying to turn the former into the latter.**

[Vincent has just removed a bullet from Sam's side]

If you don't mind, I'm gonna pass out.

—SAM, *Ronin* (1998)

☞ **Always ask permission before getting bloodstains on a coworker's office carpet.**

How do you do, sir? I, uh, I'd like to talk with you sometime, sir, and tell you about my idea for harnessing the life force. It'll make atomic power look like the horse and buggy. I'm already developing my faculty for seeing millions of miles. And Senator, can you imagine being able to smell a flower . . . on the planet Mars? I'd like to, uh, have lunch with you someday soon, sir, tell you more about it.

—BRUNO ANTHONY, *Strangers on a Train* (1951)

☞ **You're going to see a lot of presentations that make about as much sense as this. When you do, just nod and pretend to take notes.**

Never hate your enemies. It affects your judgment.

—MICHAEL CORLEONE, *The Godfather III* (1990)

☞ **Not to mention your aim.**

Who put this thing together? Me. That's who! Who do I trust? Me!

—TONY MONTANA, *Scarface* (1983)

☞ **The classic retort for anyone who asks why you can't "let go" of a project.**

When they come, they'll come at what you love.

—MICHAEL CORLEONE, *The Godfather III* (1990)

☞ **No matter how much you love your pet project, at the proper moment it may have to be euthanized for the good of everyone.**

All I can say is, they did right by me—and I'm bringin' me a mess of flowers to their funeral.

—FARMER, *Bonnie and Clyde* (1967)

☞ **Gratitude is harder to express to the living.**

[Sam accepts a cigarette offered by Vincent]

SAM: You labor or management?

VINCENT: If I was management, I would not have given you a cigarette.

—*Ronin* (1998)

☞ **He'd ask for an ashtray—and he wouldn't say please.**

The higher I go, the crookeder it becomes.

—MICHAEL CORLEONE, *The Godfather III* (1990)

☞ **And the more important it is to keep on the straight and narrow.**

People are being cheated, robbed, murdered, raped. And that goes on twenty-four hours a day, every day in the year. And that's not exceptional, that's usual. It's the same in every city in the modern world. But suppose we had no police force, good or bad. Suppose we had . . . just silence. Nobody to listen, nobody to answer. The battle's finished. The jungle wins. The predatory beasts take over.

—POLICE COMMISSIONER HARDY,
  The Asphalt Jungle (1950)

☞ **And that's not half as bad as a hostile takeover.**

My father taught me many things here. He taught me in this room.

He taught me: Keep your friends close, but your enemies closer.

—MICHAEL CORLEONE, *The Godfather II* (1974)

☞ **Make sure you and your enemy sit on the same company committees.**

Treachery is everywhere.

—DON ALTOBELLO, *The Godfather III* (1990)

☞ **No explanation necessary.**

A favor gonna kill you faster than a bullet.

—CARLITO, *Carlito's Way* (1993)

☞ **With a good deal more pain, too.**

Finance is a gun. Politics is knowing when to pull the trigger.

—DON LUCCHESI, *The Godfather III* (1990)

☞ **Often the best offense is through the budget.**

Chapter 8
BUSINESS ETHICS

I don't give a tuppenny fuck about your moral conundrum, you meat-headed shitsack!

—BILL THE BUTCHER, *Gangs of New York* (2002)

☞ **Ethical disagreements with coworkers must be handled delicately.**

I don't mind if you don't like my manners, I don't like 'em myself. They're pretty bad. I grieve over them long winter evenings.

—PHILIP MARLOWE, *The Big Sleep* (1946)

☞ **Just because you're in business doesn't mean you have to give up your conscience.**

We call it earning a living. You may have heard of it somewhere.

—JEFF BAILEY, *Out of the Past* (1947)

☛ **Not if you're the boss's brother-in-law.**

I have forsworn myself. I have broken every law I swore to defend, I have become what I beheld, and I am content that I have done right!

—ELIOT NESS, *The Untouchables* (1987)

☛ **Rules are made to be broken . . . and occasionally, so are skulls.**

BILL THE BUTCHER: Anything in your pockets?

JENNY: I ain't started working yet.

—*Gangs of New York* (2002)

☞ **By their loot shall ye know them.**

For God's sake, we bend more rules than the Catholic Church.

—JOHNNY SACK, *The Sopranos* ("The Weight," Season 4)

☞ **Which is fine, just so long as you're not breaking them.**

It's not personal, Sonny. It's strictly business.

—MICHAEL CORLEONE, *The Godfather* (1972)

☞ **And it's business even if the other guy *thinks* it's personal.**

EDIE: Shouldn't everybody care about everybody else?

TERRY MALLOY: Boy, what a fruitcake you are!

—*On the Waterfront* (1954)

☞ **And a fruitcake is something nobody wants, even at Christmas.**

Business is bad? Fuck you, pay me. Oh, you had a fire? Fuck you, pay me. The place got hit by lightning, huh? Fuck you, pay me.

—HENRY HILL, *Goodfellas* (1990)

☞ **The three most important words in business: Collect, collect, collect.**

EDIE: Which side are you with?

TERRY MALLOY: Me? I'm with me, Terry.

—*On the Waterfront* (1954)

☞ **The truth is, in business there are three people whose side you must be on: Me, myself, and I.**

[Ness has just shot a gangster]

ELIOT NESS: I had to kill him.

JIM MALONE: Oh, yeah. He's as dead as Julius Caesar . . .
Would you rather it was you?

ELIOT NESS: No, I would not.

JIM MALONE: Well, then, you've done your duty. Go home
and sleep well tonight.

—*The Untouchables* (1987)

☞ **Work will ruin some of your days; don't let
it ruin your nights, too.**

Back home they put me in jail for what I'm doing. But out here they give me awards.

—ACE ROTHSTEIN, *Casino* (1995)

☞ **Remember: The key word in the phrase "business ethics" is "business," not "ethics."**

Don't worry, I'm not going to shoot you, Mr. Haines. It might disturb Mother.

—BRUNO ANTHONY, *Strangers on a Train* (1951)

☞ **It's no crime to be considerate.**

RALPHIE CIFARETTO: Strength and honor!

ANTHONY "TONY" SOPRANO, SR.: Scotch and soda!

—*The Sopranos* ("Employee of the Month," Season 3)

☞ **Make sure your priorities are in order.**

I got sent for. In our thing, you get sent for, you go in alive, you come out dead, and it's your best friend that does it.

—LEFTY, *Donnie Brasco* (1997)

☞ **In business, you have no best friends, only "associates."**

Don't start trying to do the right thing, boy-o. You haven't had the practice.

—CAPTAIN DUDLEY SMITH, *L.A. Confidential* (1997)

☞ **As Clint put it: "A man's got to know his limitations."**

The appearance of law must be upheld, especially when it's being broken.

—BOSS TWEED, *Gangs of New York* (2002)

☞ **And if no law appears to be broken, you must not really be in business!**

You wanna waste my time? Okay. I call my lawyer. He's the best lawyer in Miami. He's such a good lawyer that by tomorrow morning you gonna be working in Alaska. So dress warm.

—TONY MONTANA, *Scarface* (1983)

☛ **Always take into account the needs of others.**

You thought you could steal from *me*?!

—BUGSY SIEGEL, *Bugsy* (1991)

☛ **Nothing wrong with stealing, so long as you make sure to steal from the right guy. A man with a name like "Bugsy" probably isn't the right guy.**

I mean, I'm very sorry the government taxes their tips, that's fucked up. That ain't my fault. I mean, it would appear that waitresses are one of the many groups the government fucks in the ass on a regular basis.

—MR. PINK, *Reservoir Dogs* (1992)

When you start feeling business ethics are hopelessly depraved, remind yourself that they're still two cuts above government ethics.

Nobody kills anybody in my place of business except me or Zed.

—MAYNARD, *Pulp Fiction* (1994)

☞ **If you don't stand for something, you'll stand for anything.**

Hey, you wanna hear my philosophy of life? Do it to him before he does it to you.

—TERRY MALLOY, *On the Waterfront* (1954)

☞ **In other words, take the golden rule and stab the guy next to you with the sharp end.**

In Italy for thirty years under the Borgias they had warfare,
terror, murder, and bloodshed, but they produced Michelangelo,
Leonardo da Vinci, and the Renaissance. In Switzerland they
had brotherly love; they had five hundred years of democracy
and peace, and what did that produce? The cuckoo clock.

—HARRY LIME, *The Third Man* (1939)

Very clever observation—until you realize
people actually buy cuckoo clocks.

Chapter 9
LEARNING FROM YOUR MISTAKES

DR. MACDONALD: Of course I'll have to notify the police.
This is a case for Homicide.

FRANK BIGELOW: Homicide!

DR. MACDONALD: I don't think you fully understand, Bigelow.
You've been murdered.

—*D.O.A.* (1949)

☞ **Try not to perform any post mortems on your own corpse.**

Every day above ground is a good day.

—BERNSTEIN, *Scarface* (1983)

☞ **On the other hand, every day underground will be a day you don't have to sit through a staff meeting.**

I'm like fucking King Midas in reverse here. Everything I touch turns to shit.

—ANTHONY "TONY" SOPRANO, SR.,
  The Sopranos ("Isabella," Season 1)

☞ **So start a compost pile!**

There's an old Italian saying: You fuck up once, you lose two teeth.

—ANTHONY "TONY" SOPRANO, SR.,

   The Sopranos ("Toodle-Fucking-Oo," Season 2)

Two or three times, you may be gumming your food.

We are protected by the enormity of your stupidity, for a time.

—MADAME SEBASTIAN, *Notorious* (1946)

If you're going to make a mistake, make it a whopper—or as Martin Luther said, "Sin boldly."

I killed him for money and for a woman. I didn't get the money,
I didn't get the woman.

—WALTER NEFF, *Double Indemnity* (1944)

☞ **On the plus side, neither one would have
brought you happiness.**

Either you're part of the problem or you're part of the solution
or you're just part of the landscape.

—SAM, *Ronin* (1998)

☞ **And if you're just part of the landscape . . .
cut your losses and get out of the picture.**

[Mr. White and Mr. Pink are washing up after the robbery went sour]

MR. PINK: Did you kill anybody?

MR. WHITE: A few cops.

MR. PINK: No real people?

MR. WHITE: Just cops.

—*Reservoir Dogs* (1992)

☞ **If you can calmly and objectively assess your failures, you're already halfway to being a wiser guy.**

POLICE CAPTAIN FINLAY: You still don't know where he is?

KEELEY: No. I didn't know when I came in here, and I haven't suddenly gotten any brighter.

—*Crossfire* (1947)

☞ **Admitting stupidity is even more dangerous than suffering from it.**

When you can't see the angles no more, you in trouble, baby.
You in trouble.

—CARLITO, *Carlito's Way* (1993)

☞ **And if you see too many angles, you're watching the receptionist instead of keeping your mind on your work.**

Maybe one reason why things are so fucked up in the organization is guys running off, not listening to middle management.

—CHRISTOPHER MOLTISANTI,
  The Sopranos ("46 Long," Season 1)

☞ **Because middle management will certainly never cop to making a mistake!**

My ass may be dumb, but I ain't no dumbass.

—ORDELL ROBBIE, *Jackie Brown* (1997)

☞ **The best way to avoid being a dumbass?
Be a smartass.**

PAULIE "WALNUTS" GUALTIER: With all the shit we've been through, you think I'll really kill you?

CHRISTOPHER MOLTISANTI: Yeah, I do.

—*The Sopranos* ("Pine Barrens," Season 3)

☞ **"Learning experiences" are a valuable team
bonding tool—but they're not a free pass.**

You know, when Khrushchev was forced out, he sat down and wrote two letters, and gave 'em to his successor. He said, uh, "When you get yourself into a situation you can't get out of, open the first letter, and you'll be safe; And when you get yourself into another situation you can't get out of, open the second letter." Well, soon enough, this guy found himself in a tight place, so he opened the first letter, which said, "Blame everything on me." So he blamed the old man, and it worked like a charm. When he got himself into a second situation he couldn't get out of, he opened the second letter, and it said, "Sit down and write two letters."

—GENERAL RALPH LANDRY, *Traffic* (2001)

So few people learn effective business correspondence until it's too late.

MICHAEL SULLIVAN, JR.: So when do I get my share of the money?

MICHAEL SULLIVAN: Well, how much do you want?

MICHAEL SULLIVAN, JR.: Two hundred dollars!

MICHAEL SULLIVAN: Okay. Deal.

MICHAEL SULLIVAN, JR.: Could I have had more?

MICHAEL SULLIVAN: You'll never know.

—*Road to Perdition* (2002)

☞ **Next time you negotiate, pick a number . . . and then add a zero to the end.**

Chapter 10

MANAGING THROUGH INTIMIDATION

You—you imbecile! You bloated idiot! You stupid fat-head!

—JOEL CAIRO, *The Maltese Falcon* (1941)

☞ **Keep job reviews short and to the point.**

You wanna talk about the rules? You wanna talk all this old-school bullshit? Well here's a rule you might remember: I am the motherfuckin'-fuckin' one who calls the shots!

—ANTHONY "TONY" SOPRANO, SR.,

  The Sopranos ("Toodle-Fucking-Oo," Season 2)

☞ **If your underlings don't seem to know who's in charge, tattoo this rule on their foreheads.**

You can get further with a kind word and a gun than you can with just a kind word.

—AL CAPONE, *The Untouchables* (1987)

☞ **And the bigger the gun, the fewer the kind words you'll need.**

Fredo, you're my older brother and I love you, but don't ever take sides with anyone against the family again. Ever.

—MICHAEL CORLEONE, *The Godfather* (1972)

☞ **Nothing is possible without loyalty.**

JAKE GITTES: There's no point in getting tough with me.
I'm just—
EVELYN MULWRAY: I don't get tough with anyone,
Mr. Gittes. My lawyer does.

—*Chinatown* (1974)

☞ **And the only thing tougher than a lawyer
is a great white shark that has been to
law school.**

[Grimsrud won't give Carl the car]

No fuckin' way! You fuckin' notice this? I got fuckin' shot. I got
fuckin' shot in the face! I went and got the fuckin' money! I got
shot fuckin' pickin' it up! I've been up for thirty-six fuckin'
hours! I'm takin' that fuckin' car! That fucker's mine!

—CARL SHOWALTER, *Fargo* (1996)

☞ **If you don't stick up for yourself, who will?**

If you hold back anything, I'll kill ya'. If you bend the truth or I think you're bending the truth, I'll kill ya'. If you forget anything, I'll kill ya'. In fact, you're gonna have to work very hard to stay alive, Nick. Now do you understand everything I've said? Because if you don't, I'll kill ya'.

—RORY BREAKER,

Lock, Stock and Two Smoking Barrels (1999)

☞ **If you can't be fair, be consistent.**

If you're going to kill somebody, do it simply.

—JOHNNIE AYSGARTH, *Suspicion* (1941)

☞ **But beware—once they're dead, you can't intimidate them into working harder.**

Cryin' department's upstairs, lady.

—GLENN GRIFFIN, *The Desperate Hours* (1955)

☞ **And in the corporate world, it's always standing room only.**

When you're slapped, you'll take it and like it.

—SAM SPADE, *The Maltese Falcon* (1941)

☞ **Make sure those reporting to you understand their duties.**

Chapter 11

BEATING THE COMPETITION—LITERALLY

EDDIE: And they're armed.

SOAP: What was that? Armed, what do you mean, armed?

EDDIE: Err, bad breath, colorful language, feather duster . . . what do you think they're gonna be armed with? Guns, you tit!

—*Lock, Stock and Two Smoking Barrels* (1999)

☞ **You need to keep abreast of the competition.**

I'm gonna get out of the car and I'm gonna drop you like third period French, okay?

—TURK MALLOY, *Ocean's Eleven* (2001)

☞ **When in doubt, blame the foreigners.**

Lesson number one: Don't underestimate the other guy's greed.

—FRANK LOPEZ, *Scarface* (1983)

☞ *You're* never satisfied—why would you think he is?

He was stupid. I was lucky. I'll visit him soon.

—MICHAEL CORLEONE, *The Godfather II* (1974)

☞ Don't ever let the competition have a second shot at you.

Jimmy was the kind of guy who rooted for the bad guys in the movies.

—HENRY HILL, *Goodfellas* (1990)

☞ **We all know what makes the bad guy bad— what you need to find out is what makes him good at it.**

My offer is this: Nothing. Not even the fee for the gaming license, which I would appreciate if you would put up personally.

—MICHAEL CORLEONE, *The Godfather II* (1974)

☞ **If you don't make outrageous demands, no one will ever meet them.**

You wanna get Capone? Here's how you get him: He pulls a knife, you pull a gun. He sends one of yours to the hospital, you send one of his to the morgue! That's the Chicago way, and that's how you get Capone! Now do you want to do that? Are you ready to do that?

—JIM MALONE, *The Untouchables* (1987)

☛ **A victory dance is always sweeter when you do it on the other guy's grave.**

BUTCH: What now?

MARSELLUS: "What now?" Let me tell you "what now." I'm 'a call a couple of hard pipe-hittin' niggers, to go to work on the homes here with a pair of pliers and a blow torch. Do you hear me talkin', hillbilly boy? I ain't through with you by a damn sight. I'm gonna get medieval on your ass.

—*Pulp Fiction* (1994)

☞ **No explanation necessary.**

[After being asked how he will arrange to buy a hotel from Moe Greene]

I'll make him an offer he can't refuse.

—MICHAEL CORLEONE, *The Godfather* (1972)

☞ **The best deal is a win-win, but if you can't get that, a simple win is also good!**

A wiseguy's always right. Even when he's wrong, he's right.

—LEFTY, *Donnie Brasco* (1997)

☞ **It's called "positive mental attitude." And if you can't manage the positive . . . make sure you've got plenty of attitude.**

In the casino, the cardinal rule is to keep them playing and to keep them coming back. The longer they play, the more they lose, and in the end, we get it all.

—ACE ROTHSTEIN, *Casino* (1995)

☛ **It's like playing strip poker—your job isn't done until everyone else is naked.**

I don't feel I have to wipe everybody out, Tom. Just my enemies.

—MICHAEL CORLEONE, *The Godfather II* (1974)

☛ **Of course when you're an enemy of humanity . . .**

I'm prepared to scour the Earth for that motherfucker. If Butch goes to Indochina, I want a nigger waiting in a bowl of rice ready to pop a cap in his ass.

—MARSELLUS, *Pulp Fiction* (1994)

☛ **Think globally, act locally.**

TERRY: I know everything that's happening in my hotels.

DANNY: So I should put those towels back?

—*Ocean's Eleven* (2001)

☛ **If you're going to steal, steal from the competition, not from the person you work for.**

No matter how big a guy might be, Nicky would take him on. You beat Nicky with fists, he comes back with a bat. You beat him with a knife, he comes back with a gun. And you beat him with a gun, you better kill him, because he'll keep comin' back and back until one of you is dead.

—ACE ROTHSTEIN, *Casino* (1995)

☞ **Competition is like comedy—it's not pretty.**

AK-47, the very best there is. When you absolutely, positively got to kill every motherfucker in the room, accept no substitutes.

—ORDELL ROBBIE, *Jackie Brown* (1997)

☞ **Branding strategies are very important if you want to "kill" the competition.**

You think you're big time? You gonna fuckin' die—big time!

—CARLITO, *Carlito's Way* (1993)

☞ **There's nothing wrong with a little friendly competition.**

I thought Mr. Clutter was a very nice gentleman. I thought so right up to the time I cut his throat.

—PERRY, *In Cold Blood* (1967)

☞ **Don't let business keep you from seeing the human side of your competition.**

It's an unlicensed boxing match, Tom, not a tickling competition. These lads are out to hurt each other.

—TURKISH, *Snatch* (2001)

☞ **If you're not inflicting enough damage on the competition, take the gloves off.**

MANNY: Oh, well what's coming to you?

TONY MONTANA: The world, chico. And everything in it.

—*Scarface* (1983)

☞ **Think big.**

Also, I think knives are a good idea. Big, fuck-off shiny ones. Ones that look like they could skin a crocodile. Knives are good, because they don't make any noise, and the less noise they make, the more likely we are to use them. Shit them right up. Makes it look like we're serious. Guns for show, knives for a pro.

—SOAP, *Lock, Stock and Two Smoking Barrels* (1999)

🔫 **And if you want to show you're a pro . . . bring both.**

He's dead now, except for he's breathing.

—DOCTOR, *The Killers* (1946)

> **Killing your competition is not enough.
> You must also cut off their oxygen.**

I'm going to paint Paradise Square with his blood. Two coats.

—BILL THE BUTCHER, *Gangs of New York* (2002)

> **To beat the competition, you must be
> prepared to work twice as hard.**

Chapter 12
DOING BUSINESS LIKE A WISEGUY

We got places all over the place.

—NICE GUY EDDIE, *Reservoir Dogs* (1992)

☞ **Be intimately familiar with all your branch offices.**

CARL SHOWALTER: I'm taking the Circa.

GAER GRIMSRUD: We split that.

CARL SHOWALTER: How the fuck do you split a fuckin' car, you dummy? With a fucking chainsaw?

—*Fargo* (1996)

☞ **You may have to get creative to cut a good deal.**

FRANK CHAMBERS: I can sell anything to anybody.

CORA SMITH: That's what you think.

—*The Postman Always Rings Twice* (1946)

☞ **Thinking makes it so.**

If you want me to keep my mouth shut, it's gonna cost you some dough. I figure a thousand bucks is reasonable, so I want two.

—TOM REAGAN, *Miller's Crossing* (1990)

☞ **When opening negotiations, ask for twice what you think you can get.**

I litigate. I don't capitulate.

—REIDENSCHNEIDER, *The Man Who Wasn't There* (2001)

☞ **There's one thing more dangerous than a loaded gun, and that's a corporate attorney.**

ALEXANDER RANCE: What do you think you're going to accomplish by interfering with our business, Mr. Sullivan?
MICHAEL SULLIVAN: This has nothing to do with your business.
ALEXANDER RANCE: It's all business. That's what you fail to grasp. And in business, you must have something to trade. And you, Mr. Sullivan, have nothing to trade.

—*Road to Perdition* (2002)

☞ **When you have nothing to trade, steal from the guy who does.**

Chapter 13
DEALING WITH CHANGE—
OR A LACK THEREOF

ANTHONY "TONY" SOPRANO, SR.: What do you got?

CHRISTOPHER MOLTISANTI: Wet shoes.

ANTHONY "TONY" SOPRANO, SR.: You chose this life. You don't want to work in the rain, try for the fucking Yankees.

—*The Sopranos* ("College," Season 1)

☞ **Accept reality.**

REPORTER: They said they're going to repeal Prohibition.
What will you do then?

ELIOT NESS: I think I'll have a drink.

—*The Untouchables* (1987)

☞ **To paraphrase Teddy Roosevelt, "Speak easy—
and carry a big cocktail."**

A minute ago this was the safest job in the world. Now it's
turning into a bad day in Bosnia.

—SOAP, *Lock, Stock and Two Smoking Barrels* (1999)

☞ **No job is ever really secure.**

The cities are full of women, middle-aged widows, husbands, dead, husbands who've spent their lives making fortunes, working and working. And then they die and leave their money to their wives, their silly wives. And what do the wives do, these useless women? You see them in the hotels, the best hotels, every day by the thousands, drinking the money, eating the money, losing the money at bridge, playing all day and all night, smelling of money, proud of their jewelry but of nothing else, horrible, faded, fat, greedy women . . . are they human or are they fat, wheezing animals, hmm? And what happens to animals when they get too fat and too old?

—UNCLE CHARLIE, *Shadow of a Doubt* (1943)

☞ **They join the board of directors.**

[After Meineke's body is dug up]

'Course he's changed some. Being buried in the earth does it.

—MR. POTTER, *The Stranger* (1946)

☞ **May all your changes be so productive and useful. As Mark Twain said, "He's no use above the ground. He should be beneath it, inspiring the cabbages."**

Just when I thought I was out, they pull me back in.

—MICHAEL CORLEONE, *The Godfather III* (1990)

☞ **Your coworkers may have trouble adjusting to your internal promotion. Make sure their trouble does not become yours.**

Now, if I ever, I mean if I *ever* see you here again, you die, just like that.

—CARLITO, *Carlito's Way* (1993)

☞ **The most effective pink slip is a black body bag.**

No money, no weed. It's all been replaced by a pile of corpses.

—TOM, *Lock, Stock and Two Smoking Barrels* (1999)

☞ **If life gives you corpses—use them for fertilizer, grow your own weed, and make all that lovely money back!**

DR. JENNIFER MELFI: Who said that after getting out of the dirt and the poverty we have to stop looking for truth and happiness?

ANTHONY "TONY" SOPRANO, SR.: Truth and happiness? Come on, I'm a fat fucking crook from New Jersey. What truth and happiness?

—*The Sopranos* ("Calling All Cars," Season 4)

☞ **Acceptance is the first step towards healing. Talking about it, however, may not make you feel any better.**

It's gettin' so a businessman can't expect no return from a fixed fight. Now, if you can't trust a fix, what can you trust? For a good return, you gotta go bettin' on chance—and then you're back with anarchy, right back in the jungle.

—JOHNNY CASPAR, *Miller's Crossing* (1990)

☞ **No, this is business—you've been in the jungle all along.**

Chapter 14
THE LAST WORD

DON CORLEONE: Do you spend time with your family?

JOHNNY FONTANE: Sure I do.

DON CORLEONE: Good. Because a man that doesn't spend time with his family can never be a real man.

—*The Godfather* (1972)

☞ **If your job is the most important thing in your life . . . get a life.**

I kill Communists for fun.

—TONY MONTANA, *Scarface* (1983)

☞ **If you can't enjoy what you do, what's the point?**

KATHIE MOFFETT: Don't, Jeff, I don't want to die!

JEFF BAILEY: Neither do I, baby, but if I have to, I'm going to die last.

—*Out of the Past* (1947)

☞ **It's never too early to start planning for retirement.**

What do ya take me for, a jumbo-sized sucker?

—WALTER BROWN, *The Narrow Margin* (1952)

☞ **Whatever they take you for, don't let them take you.**

Let's drink to Danny's honor, let's wake him to God, and hope that he gets to Heaven at least an hour before the Devil finds out he's dead.

—JOHN ROONEY, *Road to Perdition* (2002)

☞ **And when you die, if the Devil comes looking for you, take advantage of his absence by taking charge of Hell.**

Leave the gun. Take the cannolis.

—CLEMENZA, *The Godfather* (1972)

☞ **The point of being successful is to enjoy it. Know when to stop fighting and savor things.**

Now, get the fuck outta here before I shove that quotation book up your fat fucking ass!

—ANTHONY "TONY" SOPRANO, SR., *The Sopranos*

ABOUT THE AUTHOR

Kurt Luchs is general manager of the American Comedy Network, a national radio syndicator. He has been writing for *The Onion*, the world's most popular humor publication and Web site, since 1996, and contributed to the best-selling line of *Onion* books.

Kurt's humor has appeared regularly at the McSweeney's Web page, and he has also written for *The New Yorker, Slate, Modern Humorist*, and *Reason*. In addition, he is a former staff writer for *Politically Incorrect with Bill Maher* and contributes to *The Late Late Show with Craig Kilborn*.

Kurt is co-founder and editor of a new literary humor Web site called The Big Jewel. Several of his pieces are slated to appear in Volume 3 of the humor anthology *Mirth of a Nation*. He lives in Milford, Connecticut, with his wife, two children, and a seemingly endless supply of deer ticks.

ACKNOWLEDGEMENTS

I want to thank everybody at becker&mayer!, especially Andy Mayer, for bringing me this project and making me an offer I couldn't refuse; and Kate Hall, for holding my hand throughout, while poking me in the back with a cattle prod. It was fun! Let's do this again sometime. Meanwhile, please don't hurt my family.

Speaking of my family, I owe everything to my wife Suzanne. Or, technically, I owe it to all of her creditors. Thanks, darling! If not for you, I could have spent my weekends sleeping. But seriously, thanks for believing in me. Not everyone I know believes in me . . . most of them simply assume they're having some kind of psychotic breakdown. Also, thanks for joining me so often in my most sacred personal ritual: watching *The Godfather* movies at least once a week. Thanks to our daughters, Nora and Jia, for filling our lives with joy and diapers and, eventually, college bills.

I thank my father and mother for imparting to me their love of writing, movies, and humor. Cheer up—if our family was not a crime family, it was only due to lack of opportunity, not ability. Also, thanks to my brothers for teaching me so much about writing. And if you think that entitles you to a share of the royalties, you should be fishing with Fredo.

Finally, thanks to the creators of the classic crime films quoted herein. If you give all the best lines to the crooks . . . you shouldn't be surprised when somebody steals them.

INDEX